Learn **-ay** Words
day, hay, jay, say, way, clay,
play, spray, stay, sway, tray 7

Learn **-ate** Words
date, gate, Kate, late, mate, rate,
crate, grate, plate, skate, state 13

Learn **-ail** Words
fail, hail, jail, mail, nail, pail, sail,
tail, quail, snail, trail 19

Learn **-ame** Words
came, fame, game, lame, name, same,
tame, blame, flame, frame, shame 25

Learn **-eep** Words
beep, deep, jeep, keep, weep,
creep, sheep, sleep, steep, sweep 31

Learn **-eeze** Words
breeze, freeze, sneeze, squeeze,
wheeze 37

Learn **-ee** Words
agree, bee, Lee, see, flee, free, glee,
knee, three, tree 43

Learn **-ine** Words
fine, line, mine, nine, pine, vine,
wine, shine, spine, twine, whine 49

Learn **-ide** Words
hide, ride, side, tide, wide, bride,
pride, slide, inside, outside 55

Learn **-ice** Words
dice, lice, mice, nice, rice, price,
slice, spice, twice 61

Learn **-old** Words
bold, cold, fold, gold, hold, mold,
sold, told, scold... 67

Learn **-ow** Words
bow, mow, row, tow, blow, crow,
glow, grow, know, slow, snow 73

Word Games 79

Answer Key 109

What's Inside and Suggestions for Use

12 decodable stories provide students with opportunities to practice grapheme–phoneme correspondences and quickly build their confidence and ability to read connected text.

The corresponding phonics and reading comprehension activities in each unit help students increase their reading vocabulary while practicing the essential phonological skills of onset and rime. Each unit follows a consistent format:

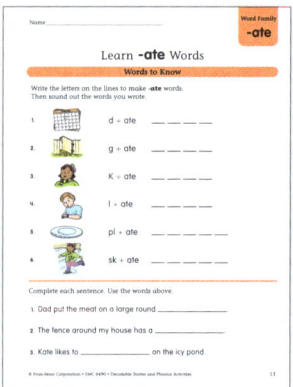

Learn Decodable Words

Model blending each initial sound with the word family phoneme. Ask students to point to each picture as they repeat the word after you. Then have students write the word family phoneme on the lines. Next, students practice reading and writing sight words from the story.

Read the Story

You may wish to have students follow along as you read the story aloud, modeling intonation and expression. Then have students read the story again, with a partner or independently.

Complete the Activity Pages

The activity page after each story focuses on reading comprehension skills. The remaining pages in the unit practice reading and writing the decodable words in context and reinforcing word meaning.

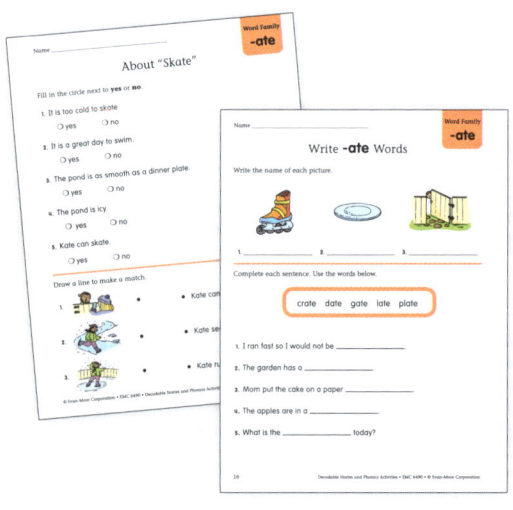

Use the Slider

The slider is a quick and easy tool that encourages repeated practice of word family vocabulary, leading to increased oral reading fluency.

4   Decodable Stories and Phonics Activities • EMC 6490 • © Evan-Moor Corporation

Decodable Stories & Phonics Activities

Book C — Grades 1-2

Editorial Development: Camille Liscinsky
Lisa Vitarisi Mathews
Jo Ellen Moore
Copy Editing: Laurie Westrich
Cover Design: Yuki Meyer
Illustration: Mary Rojas
Design/Production: Jessica Onken

EMC 6490

Congratulations on your purchase of some of the finest teaching materials in the world.

Printing or photocopying these pages is permitted for single-classroom use only. Making photocopies or sharing electronically with others is prohibited.

For information about other Evan-Moor products, call 1-800-777-4362, fax 1-800-777-4332, or visit our website, www.evan-moor.com.
Entire contents © 2024 Evan-Moor Corporation
10 Harris Court, Suite C-3, Monterey, CA 93940-5773. Printed in India.

CPSIA: Manipal Technologies Limited, Manipal, India [12/2024]

Alignment to Science of Reading

Science of Reading strategies include explicitly teaching phonics skills first and then reading decodable passages that align with those taught sounds, allowing students to practice decoding newly learned letter-sound relationships in a controlled text. Following up decodable passages with targeted reading comprehension questions and activities further supports students' literacy.

Decodable stories align with Science of Reading strategies by:

Reinforcing phonics skills

Decodable books help students practice phonics skills in a structured way.

Building confidence

Students feel a sense of accomplishment when they decode words, which boosts their confidence.

Improving fluency

Repeated practice with decodable books helps students read more quickly and accurately.

Reducing cognitive load

Decodable books limit the number of irregular words, allowing students to focus on decoding.

Helping struggling readers

Decodable books can help struggling readers and those with dyslexia by providing a predictable learning experience.

Helping students apply phonics skills

Decodable books help students apply what they learn during phonics lessons to read unfamiliar words.

Name _____

Word Family
-ay

Learn -ay Words

Words to Know

Write the letters on the lines to make -**ay** words.
Then sound out the words you made.

1.  j + ay   ___ ___ ___

2.  h + ay   ___ ___ ___

3.  cl + ay   ___ ___ ___ ___

4.  pl + ay   ___ ___ ___ ___

5.  sw + ay   ___ ___ ___ ___

6.  spr + ay ___ ___ ___ ___ ___

Complete each sentence. Use the words above.

1. My horse eats dry grass, or _____.

2. I like to _____ music while I draw.

3. Can you _____ the flowers with the garden hose?

© Evan-Moor Corporation • EMC 6490 • Decodable Stories and Phonics Activities

Story words to know: hose, crayons, form, music, barn

Name _____

Word Family -ay

Read -ay Words

Read the story.

A Day of Fun

Come this way.
Have some fun!
Spray with a hose.
Run in the sun.

Get some crayons.
Take some clay.
Make a drawing.
Form a blue jay.

Play some music.
Sing and sway.
Find the red barn.
Jump in the hay.

What do you say?
You want to stay.
Hip, hip, hooray!

Take the story home. Read it to your family.

Name _____

Word Family
-ay

About "A Day of Fun"

Circle the word that tells about the story. Then write the word on the line.

1. Form a blue jay with _____.   gray   clay

2. Jump in the _____.   hay   ham

3. Use a hose to _____.   stay   spray

4. _____ some music.   Play   Pull

5. Dance and _____ to the music.   sway   swim

Fill in the circle next to the correct answer.

1. What is a good name for the story?
    - ○ The Sad Day
    - ○ A Day to Play

2. Where is the hay?
    - ○ in the barn
    - ○ on a tray

3. What is a word that means **happy**?
    - ○ hooray
    - ○ boo

© Evan-Moor Corporation • EMC 6490 • Decodable Stories and Phonics Activities

Name _____

Write -ay Words

Word Family -ay

Fill in the circle next to the name of each picture.

1.
   - ○ ham
   - ○ may
   - ○ hay

2.
   - ○ clay
   - ○ day
   - ○ spray

3.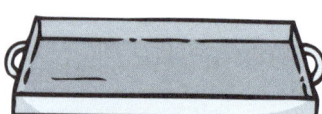
   - ○ they
   - ○ tray
   - ○ the

Complete each sentence. Use the words below.

> gray   play   say   Today   way

1. Matt likes to _____ tag.

2. The sky is _____ when it rains.

3. He will show me the _____ to the barn.

4. I hope Mom will _____ yes.

5. _____ is a fun day.

10   Decodable Stories and Phonics Activities • EMC 6490 • © Evan-Moor Corporation

Note: Cut out the slider parts along the dashed lines. Then slip the word strip through the slider window.

Word Family -ay

Slide and Read

↑ Pull Up

day

hay

jay

say

way

clay

play

spray

stay

sway

tray

Practice **-ay** Words

I know these words!

Hooray!

© Evan-Moor Corporation • EMC 6490 • Decodable Stories and Phonics Activities

end of
-ay words

day hay jay say way clay play spray stay tray day sway tray jay hay say

Name _____

Word Family
-ate

Learn -ate Words

Words to Know

Write the letters on the lines to make **-ate** words.
Then sound out the words you wrote.

1.  d + ate   ___ ___ ___ ___

2.  g + ate   ___ ___ ___ ___

3.  K + ate   ___ ___ ___ ___

4.  l + ate   ___ ___ ___ ___

5.  pl + ate ___ ___ ___ ___ ___

6.  sk + ate ___ ___ ___ ___ ___

Complete each sentence. Use the words above.

1. Dad put the meat on a large round _____.

2. The fence around my house has a _____.

3. Kate likes to _____ on the icy pond.

© Evan-Moor Corporation • EMC 6490 • Decodable Stories and Phonics Activities

Story words to know: icy, great, pond, smooth, dinner

Word Family -ate

Name _____

Read -ate Words

Read the story.

Skate

The day is cold.
The day is icy.
"What a great day!" says Kate.

She runs down the path.
Kate sees her friend at the gate.
She isn't too late for the fun.

The pond shines.
It looks as smooth as a dinner plate.
Kate pushes off.
Around and around she begins to skate.

Take the story home. Read it to your family.

14 Decodable Stories and Phonics Activities • EMC 6490 • © Evan-Moor Corporation

Name _____

Word Family -ate

About "Skate"

Fill in the circle next to **yes** or **no**.

1. It is too cold to skate.

   ○ yes ○ no

2. It is a great day to swim.

   ○ yes ○ no

3. The pond is as smooth as a dinner plate.

   ○ yes ○ no

4. The pond is icy.

   ○ yes ○ no

5. Kate can skate.

   ○ yes ○ no

Draw a line to make a match.

1.  • • Kate can skate.

2.  • • Kate sees her friend at the gate.

3.  • • Kate runs down the path.

© Evan-Moor Corporation • EMC 6490 • Decodable Stories and Phonics Activities 15

Name_____

Word Family -ate

Write **-ate** Words

Write the name of each picture.

1. _____   2. _____   3. _____

Complete each sentence. Use the words below.

> crate   date   gate   late   plate

1. I ran fast so I would not be _____.

2. The garden has a _____.

3. Mom put the cake on a paper _____.

4. The apples are in a _____.

5. What is the _____ today?

Note: Cut out the slider parts along the dashed lines. Then slip the word strip through the slider window.

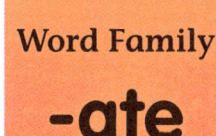

Slide and Read

↑ Pull Up

date

gate

Kate

late

mate

rate

crate

grate

plate

skate

state

Practice -ate Words

I know these words!

Hooray!

date gate Kate
late mate
rate
end of
-ate words
crate
grate
plate
date
skate state
Kate
gate late

Name _____

Word Family -ail

Learn -ail Words

Words to Know

Write the letters on the lines to make **-ail** words.
Then sound out the words you wrote.

1.    m + ail   ___ ___ ___

2.    s + ail   ___ ___ ___

3.    t + ail   ___ ___ ___

4.    qu + ail   ___ ___ ___ ___

5.    sn + ail   ___ ___ ___ ___

6.    tr + ail   ___ ___ ___ ___

Complete each sentence. Use the words above.

1. A _____ makes a _____ of slime when it moves.

2. A _____ has _____ feathers.

© Evan-Moor Corporation • EMC 6490 • Decodable Stories and Phonics Activities   19

Story words to know: send, today, can't, when

Word Family -ail

Name _____

Read **-ail** Words

Read the story.

The Snail and the Quail

"Send me some mail,"
    said the snail to the quail.
"Send me some mail today."

"I can't send you mail,"
    said the quail to the snail.
"Today I sail away."

"Look for my trail,"
    said the snail to the quail.
"When you get back, we will play."

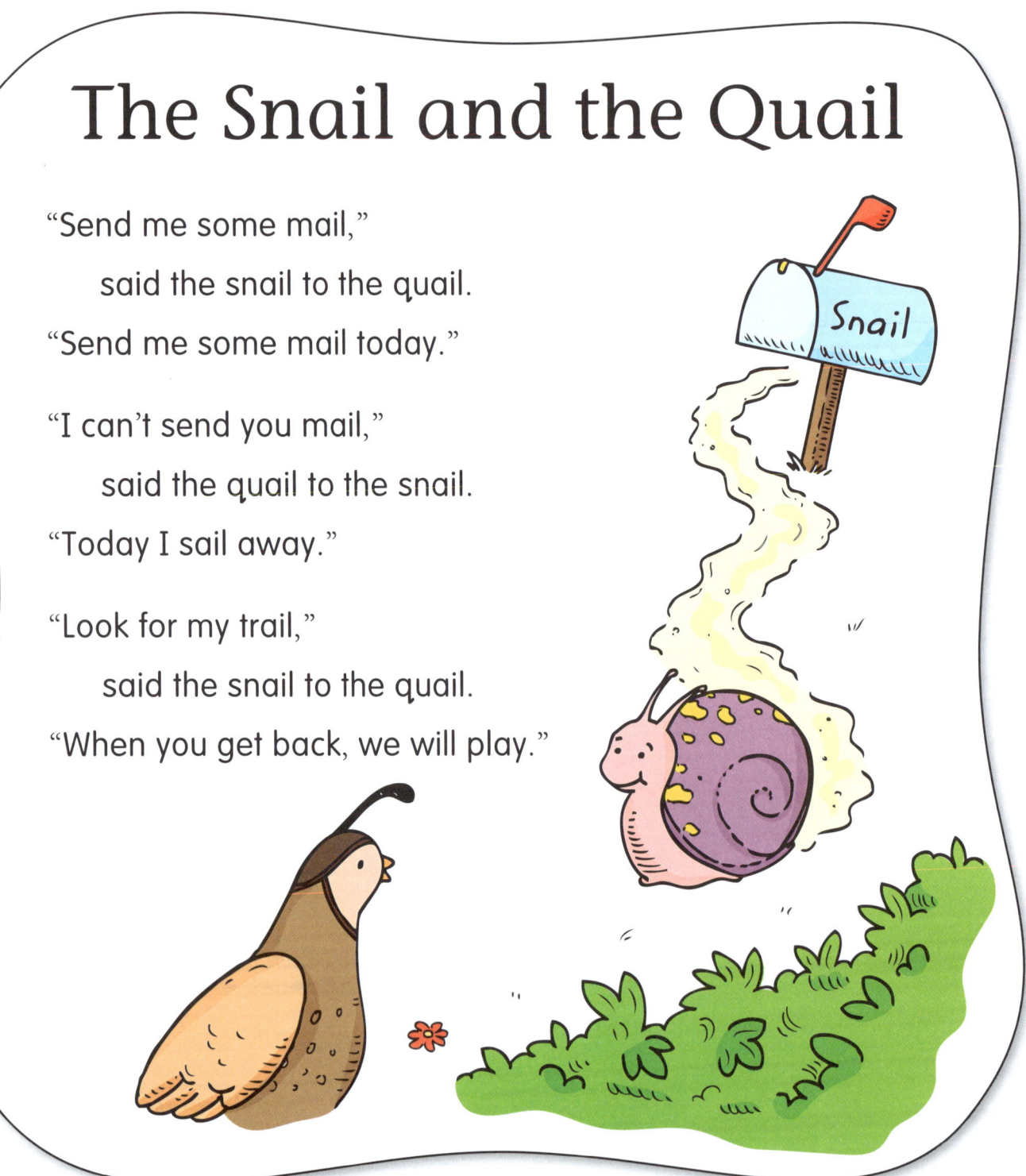

Take the story home. Read it to your family.

Name _____

Word Family -ail

About "The Snail and the Quail"

Fill in the circle that tells about the story.

1. Who wants mail?

    ○ the snail
    ○ the quail
    ○ the trail

2. Who can't send mail?

    ○ the snail
    ○ the quail
    ○ the trail

3. Why can't the quail send mail?

    ○ The quail is going away.
    ○ The quail is on a bus.
    ○ The quail cannot read.

4. How will the quail find the snail?

    ○ The snail will make a trail.
    ○ The snail will mail the quail.
    ○ The snail will yell.

5. What will the snail and the quail do when the quail gets back?

    ○ They will sail away.
    ○ They will play.
    ○ They will eat.

Name _____

Word Family
-ail

Write -ail Words

Write the name of each picture.

1. _____ 2. _____ 3. _____

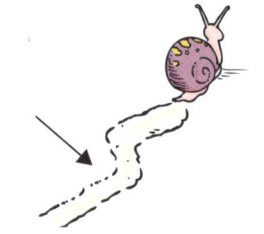 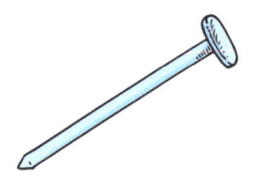 

4. _____ 5. _____ 6. _____

Complete each sentence. Use the words above.

1. A _____ is a bird.

2. A _____ is slow.

3. Mom hit the _____ with the hammer.

4. Gail put the card in the _____.

5. My dog can wag its _____.

6. A snail makes a _____.

22 Decodable Stories and Phonics Activities • EMC 6490 • © Evan-Moor Corporation

Note: Cut out the slider parts along the dashed lines.
Then slip the word strip through the slider window.

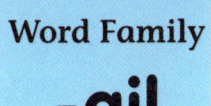

Word Family
-ail

Slide and Read

↑ Pull Up

fail

hail

jail

mail

nail

pail

sail

tail

quail

snail

trail

Practice **-ail** Words

I know these words!

Hooray!

end of
-ail words

Name _____

Word Family
-ame

Learn -ame Words

Words to Know

Write the letters on the lines to make -**ame** words.
Then sound out the words you wrote.

1.  g + ame   ___ ___ ___ ___

2.  s + ame   ___ ___ ___ ___

3.  t + ame   ___ ___ ___ ___

4.  fl + ame ___ ___ ___ ___ ___

5.  fr + ame ___ ___ ___ ___ ___

Complete each sentence. Use the words above.

1. We can play my new computer _____.

2. A lion is wild, not _____.

3. My art hangs in a _____.

Read these -**ame** words.

came   lame   shame

Story words to know: never, bears, brave, fire, draws

Word Family -ame

Name _____

Read -ame Words

Read the story.

The Game

Every day, James makes up a game.
The game is never the same.

James sees bears.
James is brave.
He can tame them.

James hears a boom.
He sees a flame!
He puts out the fire.

James draws.
He uses many colors.
James puts his art in a big frame.

James plays fun games.

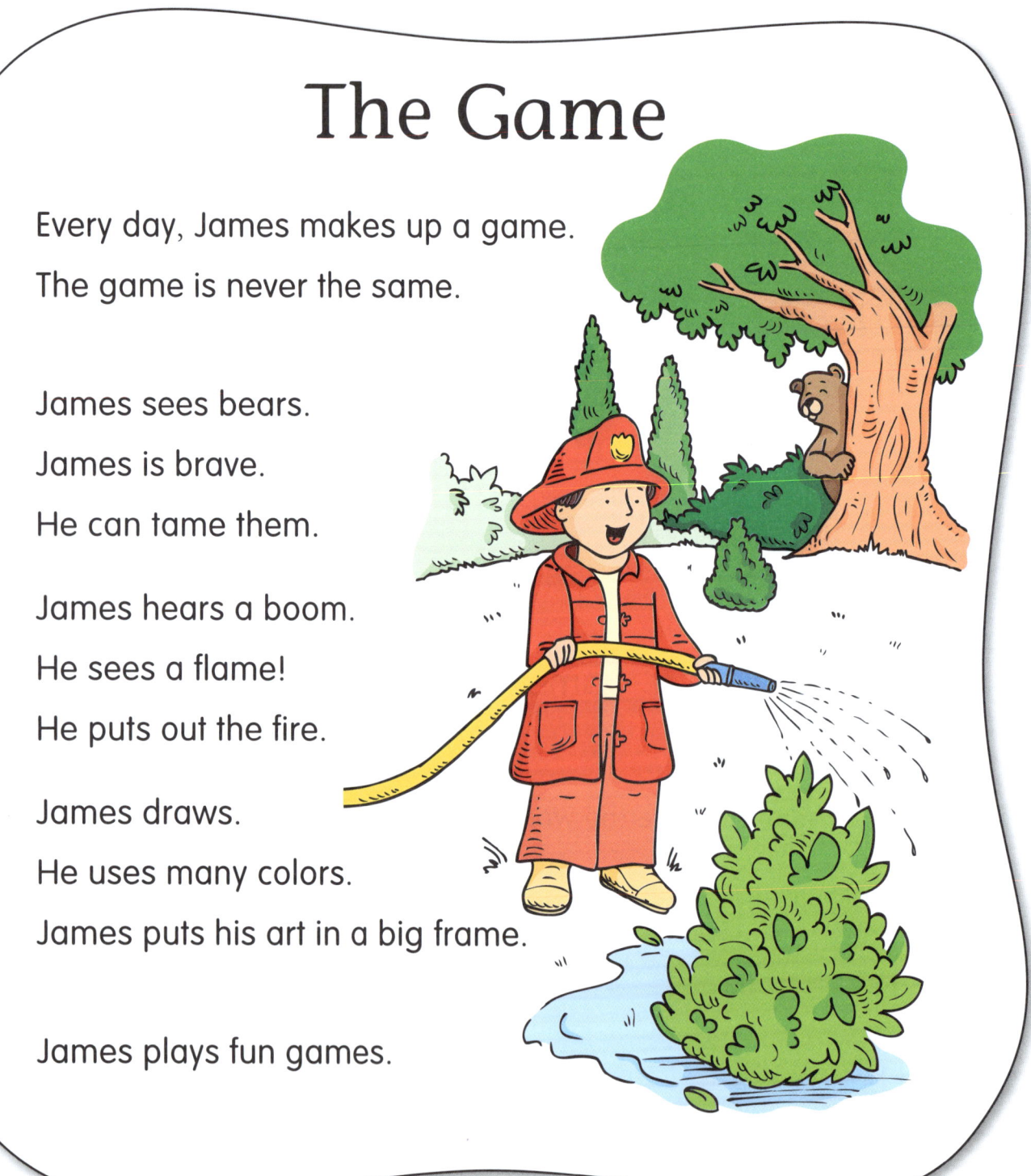

Take the story home. Read it to your family.

26 Decodable Stories and Phonics Activities • EMC 6490 • © Evan-Moor Corporation

Name _____

Word Family

-ame

About "The Game"

Fill in the circle that tells about the story.

1. What is the story about?

    ○ James sings.
    ○ James makes up games.
    ○ James does not like to play games.

2. What does James do to the bears?

    ○ James names the bears.
    ○ James feeds the bears.
    ○ James tames the bears.

3. James sees a flame. He _____.

    ○ watches the fire
    ○ puts out the fire
    ○ puts a log on the fire

4. Where does James put his art?

    ○ in a box
    ○ in a frame
    ○ on the wall

5. Which one tells about James?

    ○ James is old.
    ○ James is sad.
    ○ James is fun.

© Evan-Moor Corporation • EMC 6490 • Decodable Stories and Phonics Activities

Name _____

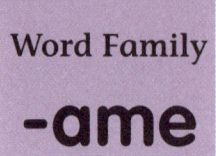

Write -ame Words

Write the name of each picture.

1. _____   2. _____   3. _____

Complete each sentence. Use the words below.

> blame   came   flame   tame

1. James _____ to see me.

2. I will _____ my pet tiger.

3. The _____ is hot.

4. I will take the _____ for this mess.

Write a sentence about a game you play. Use the word **game**.

_____
_____
_____.

28 Decodable Stories and Phonics Activities • EMC 6490 • © Evan-Moor Corporation

Note: Cut out the slider parts along the dashed lines.
Then slip the word strip through the slider window.

Word Family -ame

Slide and Read

Pull Up ↑

came

fame

game

lame

name

same

tame

blame

flame

frame

shame

Practice -ame Words

I know these words!

Hooray!

end of
-ame words

Name _____

Word Family
-eep

Learn -eep Words

Words to Know

Write the letters on the lines to make **-eep** words.
Then sound out the words you made.

1.  d + eep   ___ ___ ___ ___

2.  cr + eep   ___ ___ ___ ___ ___

3.  sh + eep   ___ ___ ___ ___ ___

4.  sl + eep   ___ ___ ___ ___ ___

5.  st + eep   ___ ___ ___ ___ ___

Complete each sentence. Use the words above.

1. That lake is very _____.

2. The hill is too _____ for me to go up.

3. The dog likes to _____ low to the ground.

Read these **-eep** words.

keep   weep   beep

Story words to know: ready, job, around, safe

Name _____

Word Family -eep

Read **-eep** Words

Read the story.

Who Cares for Sheep?

The dog is not ready to sleep.

He has a job.

He cares for sheep.

The dog can creep low.

He can run around the sheep.

He makes them stay in the grass.

The sheep stay away from steep land.

They will not go into deep water.

The dog will keep the sheep safe.

Take the story home. Read it to your family.

Name_____

Word Family -eep

About "Who Cares for Sheep?"

Fill in the circle that tells about the story.

1. What is the story about?
    - ○ a dog and cat
    - ○ sheep
    - ○ a dog and sheep

2. Where is a good place for sheep?
    - ○ in deep water
    - ○ on steep land
    - ○ in grass

3. What do sheep eat?
    - ○ grass
    - ○ land
    - ○ dogs

Draw a line to make a match.

1. • • The dog keeps the sheep safe.

2. • • The sheep eat grass.

3. • • The dog can creep.

© Evan-Moor Corporation • EMC 6490 • Decodable Stories and Phonics Activities

Name _____

Write -eep Words

Word Family -eep

Write the name of each picture.

1. _____ 2. _____ 3. _____

4. _____ 5. _____ 6. _____

Complete each sentence. Use the words below.

> deep   keep   sheep   sweep

1. The dog cares for the _____.

2. Mom and Dad _____ me safe.

3. Jen will _____ away the dirt.

4. Jon does not swim in _____ water.

34   Decodable Stories and Phonics Activities • EMC 6490 • © Evan-Moor Corporation

Note: Cut out the slider parts along the dashed lines. Then slip the word strip through the slider window.

Word Family -eep

Slide and Read

↑ Pull Up

beep

deep

jeep

keep

weep

creep

sheep

sleep

steep

sweep

Practice -eep Words

I know these words! Hooray!

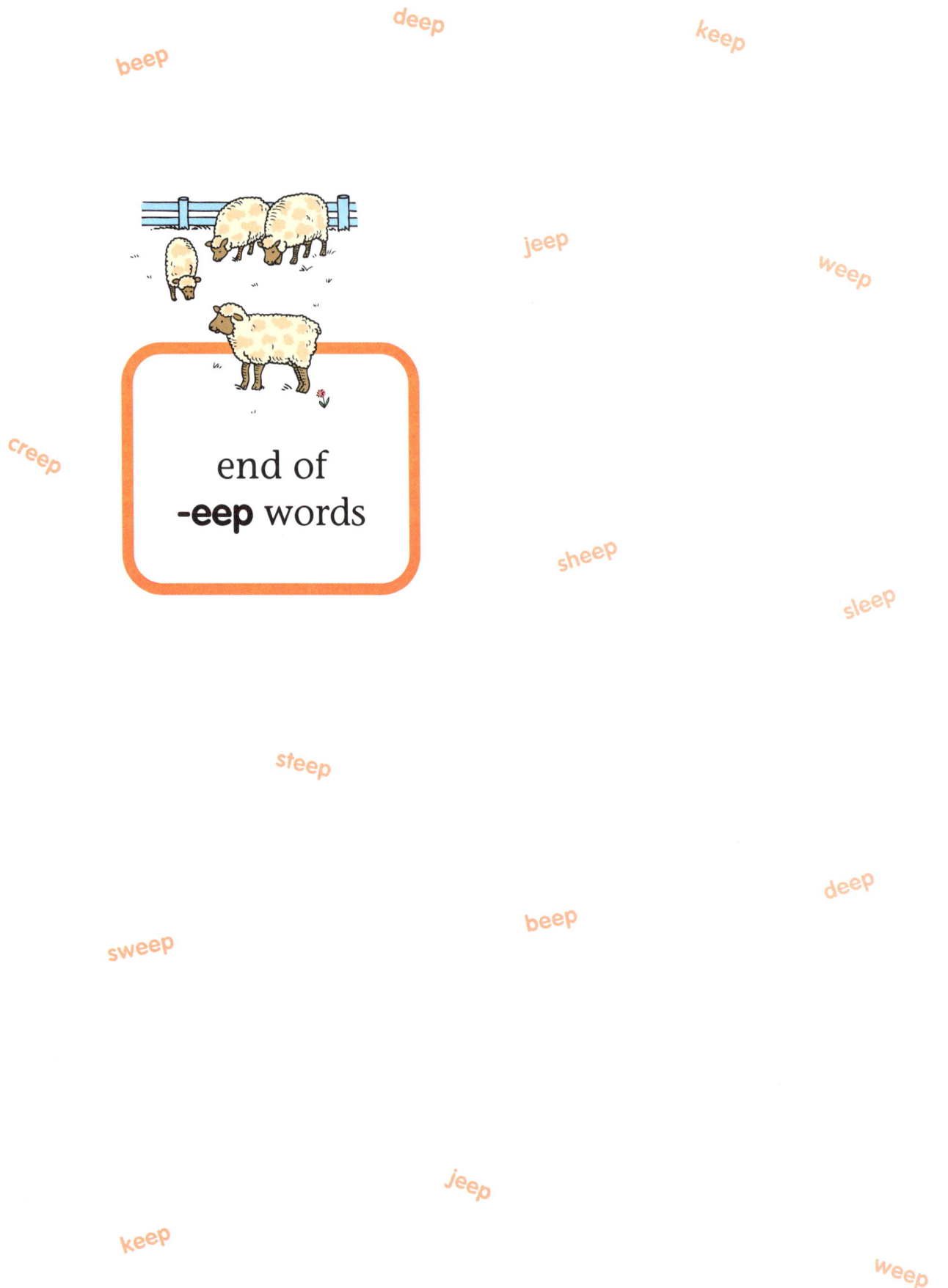

Name _____

Word Family
-eeze

Learn **-eeze** Words

Words to Know

Write the letters on the lines to make **-eeze** words.
Then sound out the words you wrote.

1.  br + eeze   __ __ __ __ __ __

2.  fr + eeze   __ __ __ __ __ __

3.  sn + eeze   __ __ __ __ __ __

4.  squ + eeze   __ __ __ __ __ __ __

Complete each sentence. Use the words above.

1. Cold air makes water _____ into ice.

2. The _____ blew the trees.

3. I _____ my bear.

4. Please cover your mouth when you _____.

Read these **-eeze** words.

wheeze   tweeze

© Evan-Moor Corporation • EMC 6490 • Decodable Stories and Phonics Activities

Story words to know: lettuce, carrots, peppers, tomato, salad

Word Family -eeze

Name _____

Read -eeze Words

Read the story.

Squeeze, Squeeze, Squeeze

You toss the lettuce

with carrots and cheese.

But…

Don't put in peppers or I'll sneeze, sneeze, sneeze.

Skip the cold tomato or I'll freeze, freeze, freeze.

Don't put in peanuts or I'll wheeze, wheeze, wheeze.

Just add some lemon

with a squeeze, squeeze, squeeze.

I bet this salad will be sure to please!

Take the story home. Read it to your family.

Name _____

Word Family
-eeze

About "Squeeze, Squeeze, Squeeze"

Complete each sentence.

1. 🥜 make the boy _____.

2. 🥬 make the boy _____.

3. A cold 🍅 makes the boy _____.

Make each sound. Draw a line to match the sounds to the words.

1. Achoo! •   • squeeze

2. Brrrr! •   • sneeze

3. Ouch! •   • freeze

Draw two things you can squeeze.

© Evan-Moor Corporation • EMC 6490 • Decodable Stories and Phonics Activities

Name _____

Word Family -eeze

Write **-eeze** Words

Complete each sentence. Use the words below.

> breeze   freeze   sneeze   squeeze

1. I will _____ the lemon.

2. Water can _____ into ice.

3. I _____ when I have a cold.

4. A _____ is a soft wind.

Write a sentence about a soft wind. Use the word **breeze**.

_____

_____.

Write a sentence about something that gets cold. Use the word **freeze**.

_____

_____.

Note: Cut out the slider parts along the dashed lines. Then slip the word strip through the slider window.

Word Family
-eeze

Slide and Read

↑ Pull Up

breeze

freeze

sneeze

squeeze

wheeze

Practice **-eeze** Words

I know these words!

Hooray!

end of
-eeze words

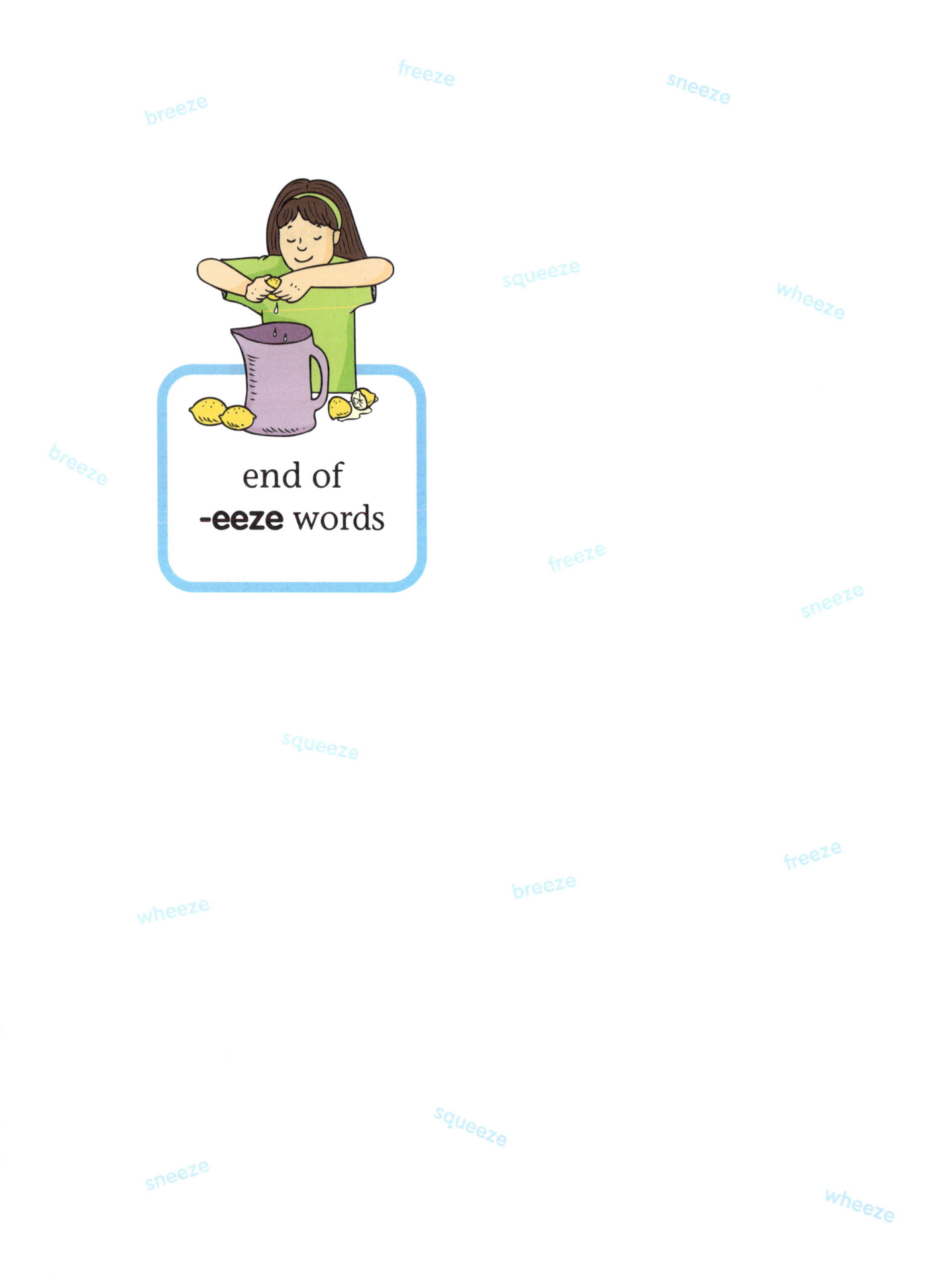

Name_____

Word Family
-ee

Learn -ee Words

Words to Know

Write the letters on the lines to make **-ee** words.
Then sound out the words you made.

1.  b + ee   ___ ___ ___

2.  fr + ee   ___ ___ ___ ___

3.  gl + ee   ___ ___ ___ ___

4.  kn + ee   ___ ___ ___ ___

5.  tr + ee   ___ ___ ___ ___

6.  thr + ee   ___ ___ ___ ___ ___

Complete each sentence. Use the words above.

1. Your _____ is part of your leg.

2. Jay picks apples from that _____.

3. A honey_____ has four wings.

© Evan-Moor Corporation • EMC 6490 • Decodable Stories and Phonics Activities

Story words to know: pal, close, together, honey

Word Family -ee

Name _____

Read -ee Words

Read the story.

You and Me

You are my pal.

We're as close as can be.

We go together

    like honey and a bee,
    like a leg and a knee,
    like a bird and a tree,
    like one, two, three!

Don't you agree?

Take the story home. Read it to your family.

Name_____

Word Family
-ee

About "You and Me"

Draw a line to make a match.

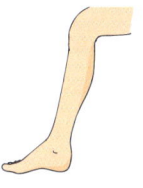

1. [honey jar] •   • tree

2. **one, two,** •   • knee

3. [leg/knee] •   • bee

4. [bird] •   • three

Fill in the circle next to **yes** or **no**.

1. The story is about friends.

    ○ yes   ○ no

2. The friends like each other.

    ○ yes   ○ no

The word **glee** means "a feeling of joy."
Trace the word **glee**. Complete the sentence with the name of a friend.

My friend _____ makes me laugh with glee.

© Evan-Moor Corporation • EMC 6490 • Decodable Stories and Phonics Activities

Name _____

Word Family
-ee

Write -ee Words

Write the name of each picture.

1. _____ 2. _____ 3. _____

Complete each sentence. Use the words below.

> agree   free   knee   see   three

1. I can bend my _____.

2. What do you _____ in the tree?

3. I _____ with what you said.

4. I see _____ bees on the flower.

5. You do not have to pay. The game is _____.

Note: Cut out the slider parts along the dashed lines.
Then slip the word strip through the slider window.

Word Family

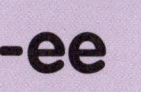

-ee

Slide and Read

↑ Pull Up

agree

bee

Lee

see

flee

free

glee

knee

three

tree

Practice **-ee** Words

I know these words!

Hooray!

end of
-ee words

Name _____

Word Family -ine

Learn -ine Words

Words to Know

Write the letters on the lines to make **-ine** words.
Then sound out the words you wrote.

1. l + ine   ___ ___ ___ ___

2. m + ine   ___ ___ ___ ___

3. n + ine   ___ ___ ___ ___

4. p + ine   ___ ___ ___ ___

5. sh + ine   ___ ___ ___ ___

6. wh + ine   ___ ___ ___ ___

Complete each sentence. Use the words above.

1. We stand in _____ to get on the school bus.

2. My brother will _____ to get his way.

3. When will the rain stop so the sun can _____?

Story words to know: trip, shook, number, first

Word Family -ine

Name _____

Read -ine Words

Read the story.

Sam Feels Fine

Sam woke up.

He saw the sun shine into his room.

Sam said, "Can I go on the school trip?"

Mom shook her head.

"You're sick," said Mom.

Sam began to whine.

"But I feel fine.

All the kids are going."

Mom gave in.

The kids got in line for the bus.

Sam was number nine in line.

Leo got on first.

"The seat by you is mine!" said Sam.

They had a great time.

Take the story home. Read it to your family.

Name_____

Word Family
-ine

About "Sam Feels Fine"

Fill in the circle next to **yes** or **no**.

1. Sam saw the rain from his room.

    ○ yes   ○ no

2. Sam whines to get his way.

    ○ yes   ○ no

3. Sam goes on a school trip.

    ○ yes   ○ no

4. Leo is number nine in line.

    ○ yes   ○ no

5. Sam and Tim sit together.

    ○ yes   ○ no

Show when each thing happened. Write **1**, **2**, **3**, **4**.

_____ The sun shines.

_____ Sam says, "The seat by you is mine!"

_____ Sam is number nine in line.

_____ Sam whines to his mom.

Name _____

Word Family -ine

Write -ine Words

Fill in the circle next to the name of each picture.

1.
- ○ like
- ○ live
- ○ line

2.
- ○ mine
- ○ pine
- ○ shine

3.
- ○ whine
- ○ fine
- ○ nine

Complete each sentence. Use the words below.

line   mine   pine   shine   spine

1. I see the stars _____.

2. That green coat is _____.

3. The bones in your back are your _____.

4. A _____ tree has cones.

5. The kids stand in _____ for the bus.

52 Decodable Stories and Phonics Activities • EMC 6490 • © Evan-Moor Corporation

Note: Cut out the slider parts along the dashed lines.
Then slip the word strip through the slider window.

Word Family -ine

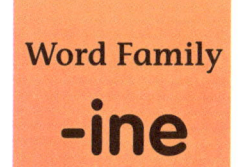

Slide and Read

↑
Pull Up

fine

line

mine

nine

pine

vine

wine

shine

spine

twine

whine

Practice -ine Words

I know these words!

Hooray!

© Evan-Moor Corporation • EMC 6490 • Decodable Stories and Phonics Activities

end of
-ine words

Name_____

Word Family
-ide

Learn **-ide** Words

Words to Know

Write the letters on the lines to make **-ide** words.
Then sound out the words you wrote.

1.  h + ide   ___ ___ ___ ___

2.  r + ide   ___ ___ ___ ___

3.  s + ide   ___ ___ ___ ___

4.  w + ide   ___ ___ ___ ___

5.  pr + ide   ___ ___ ___ ___ ___

6.  sl + ide   ___ ___ ___ ___ ___

Complete each sentence. Use the words above.

1. The kitten stays close to its mother's _____.

2. My cat likes to _____ under the couch.

3. A cat can open its mouth very _____.

© Evan-Moor Corporation • EMC 6490 • Decodable Stories and Phonics Activities

Story words to know: lion, zoo, hunt, mouth

Word Family -ide

Name _____

Read **-ide** Words

Read the story.

A Pride of Lions

A lion is a very big cat.
Some lions live inside a zoo.
Most lions live outside.

They hunt for food.
A lion opens its mouth very wide.
It takes big bites.

The fur of a lion is yellow-brown.
The color helps a lion hide in dry grass.

Some lions live together.
They are called a pride.

A baby lion stays near its mother's side.
She keeps the cub safe.

Take the story home. Read it to your family.

Name _____

Word Family -ide

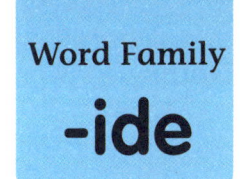

About "A Pride of Lions"

Fill in the circle next to the correct answer. Write the word on the line.

1. Some lions live inside a _____.

    ○ zoo
    ○ house
    ○ grass

2. When lions live together, they are called a _____.

    ○ hide
    ○ bride
    ○ pride

3. A baby lion is called a _____.

    ○ kitten
    ○ cub
    ○ puppy

Draw a line to make a match.

1. • • A cub stays by its mother's side.

2. • • A lion can hide in dry grass.

3. • • A lion can open its mouth wide.

© Evan-Moor Corporation • EMC 6490 • Decodable Stories and Phonics Activities

Name _____

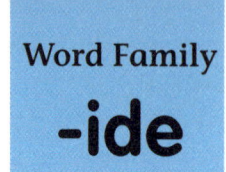

Word Family -ide

Write -ide Words

Complete each sentence. Use the words below.

> hide   inside   ride   side   slide

1. I like to _____ my bike.

2. My dog likes to _____ his bone.

3. Do you like to play _____ or outside?

4. The ice makes me slip and _____.

5. The cub is at its mother's _____.

Write a sentence about a park. Use the word **slide**.

_____

_____

Write a sentence about a bus. Use the word **ride**.

_____

_____

Note: Cut out the slider parts along the dashed lines. Then slip the word strip through the slider window.

Word Family -ide

Slide and Read

↑ Pull Up

hide

ride

side

tide

wide

bride

pride

slide

inside

outside

Practice -ide Words

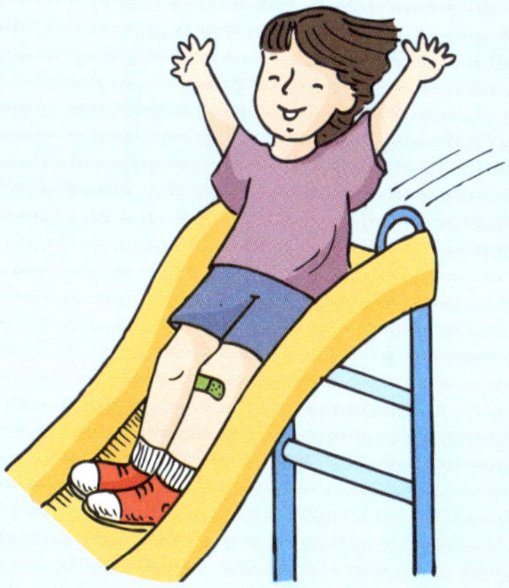

I know these words!

Hooray!

end of
-ide words

Name_____

Word Family -ice

Learn -ice Words

Words to Know

Write the letters on the lines to make **-ice** words.
Then sound out the words you wrote.

1. d + ice   ___ ___ ___ ___
2. m + ice   ___ ___ ___ ___
3. n + ice   ___ ___ ___ ___
4. r + ice   ___ ___ ___ ___
5. pr + ice   ___ ___ ___ ___ ___

Complete each sentence. Use the words above.

1. You need to roll the _____ to play.

2. We eat _____ for dinner.

3. The _____ of the coat is too high.

Read these **-ice** words.

twice   lice   spice

Story words to know: roll, highest, pile, lowest

Word Family -ice

Name _____

Read -ice Words

Read the story.

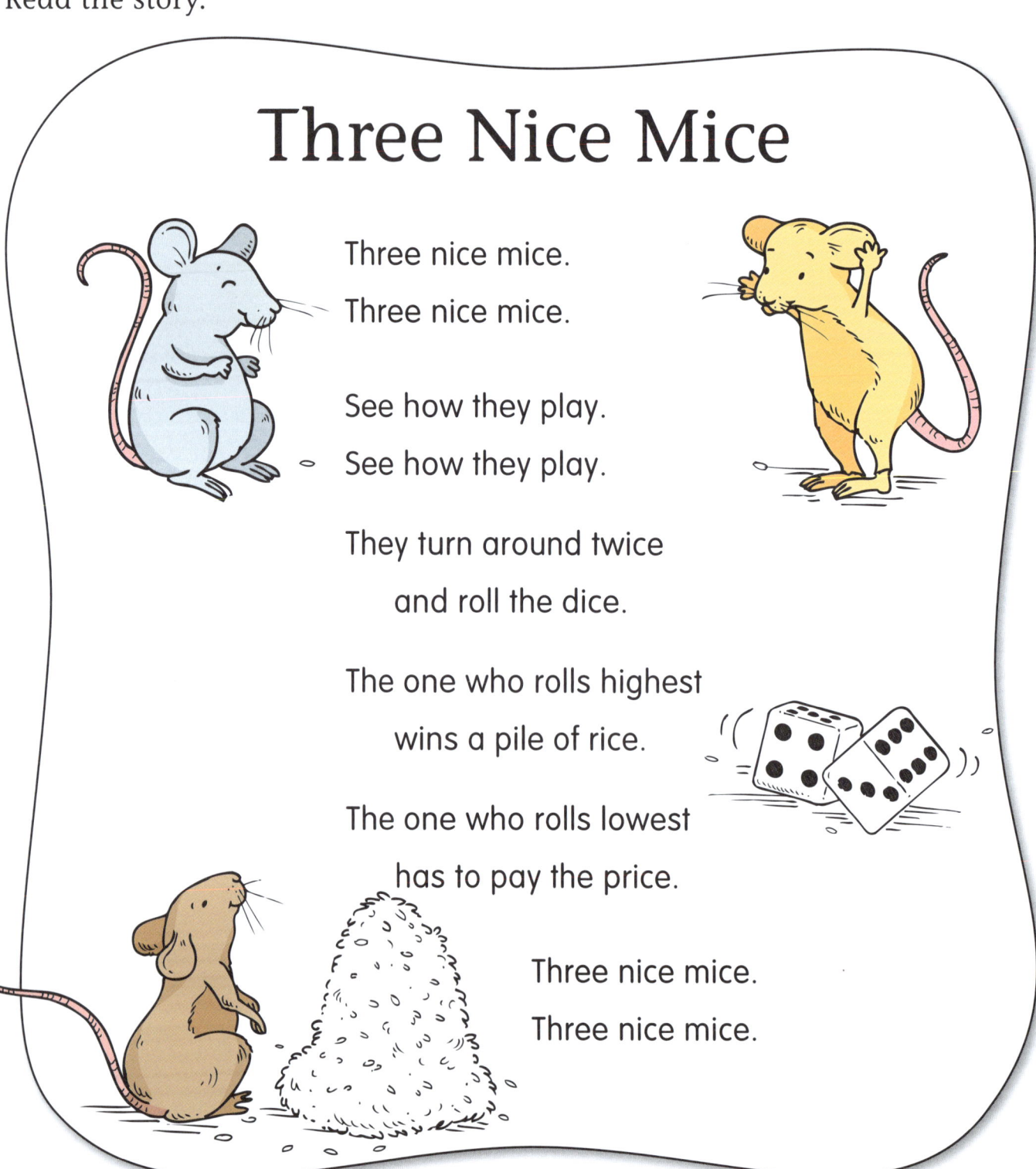

Three Nice Mice

Three nice mice.
Three nice mice.

See how they play.
See how they play.

They turn around twice
and roll the dice.

The one who rolls highest
wins a pile of rice.

The one who rolls lowest
has to pay the price.

Three nice mice.
Three nice mice.

Take the story home. Read it to your family.

Name _____

Word Family
-ice

About "Three Nice Mice"

Fill in the circle that tells about the story.

1. Who?
   - ○ two little mice
   - ○ one nice mouse
   - ○ three nice mice

2. What?
   - ○ play a game of dice
   - ○ play tag
   - ○ eat rice

3. Why?
   - ○ to win a slice of pie
   - ○ to win a pile of rice
   - ○ to win a pile of ice

Fill in the circle next to **yes** or **no**.

1. The story tells about real mice.
   - ○ yes   ○ no

2. The mice like to play with dice.
   - ○ yes   ○ no

3. The mice like to eat rice.
   - ○ yes   ○ no

Name _____

Word Family -ice

Write -ice Words

Write the name of each picture.

1. _____   2. _____   3. _____

Complete each sentence. Use the words below.

> dice   nice   price   rice   slice

1. Mom cooks the _____ in a pot.

2. We play the game with two _____.

3. Dad put jam on the _____ of bread.

4. You are a _____ friend.

5. Look at the tag to see the _____.

64   Decodable Stories and Phonics Activities • EMC 6490 • © Evan-Moor Corporation

Note: Cut out the slider parts along the dashed lines. Then slip the word strip through the slider window.

Word Family -ice

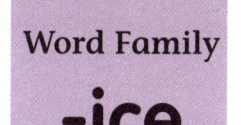

Slide and Read

↑ Pull Up

dice

lice

mice

nice

rice

price

slice

spice

twice

Practice -ice Words

I know these words!

Hooray!

© Evan-Moor Corporation • EMC 6490 • Decodable Stories and Phonics Activities

end of
-ice words

Name_____

Word Family
-old

Learn -old Words

Words to Know

Write the letters on the lines to make **-old** words.
Then sound out the words you wrote.

1.  c + old   ___ ___ ___ ___

2.  g + old   ___ ___ ___ ___

3.  h + old   ___ ___ ___ ___

4.  t + old   ___ ___ ___ ___

5.  sc + old   ___ ___ ___ ___ ___

Complete each sentence. Use the words above.

1. I _____ my puppy when he chews on my shoe.

2. The puppy likes to splash in _____ water.

3. My puppy is the color of _____.

Read these **-old** words.

bold   mold   fold

Story words to know: wrong, should, splash, afraid

Word Family -old

Name _____

Read **-old** Words

Read the story.

What Can It Be?

One thing is wrong with my puppy.
She does not have a name.

Her fur is gold.
I can call her Sunny.

She likes when I hold her.
Should I call her Hugs?

I scold her when she bites.
Is Jaws a good name?

She likes cold water.
I can call her Splash.

She is bold and not afraid.
Should I call her Brave?

Can you think of a good name?

Take the story home. Read it to your family.

Name _____

Word Family -old

About "What Can It Be?"

Fill in the circle that tells about the story.

1. What is wrong with the puppy?

    ○ She is sick.
    ○ She is old.
    ○ She needs a name.

2. Why is Jaws a good name?

    ○ The puppy likes to bite.
    ○ The puppy has gold fur.
    ○ The puppy likes to play.

3. What does it mean to be **bold**?

    ○ to be big
    ○ to be little
    ○ to be brave

Draw a line to tell why the name is good.

1. Brave •   • The puppy has gold fur.

2. Splash •   • The puppy is bold.

3. Sunny •   • The puppy likes cold water.

© Evan-Moor Corporation • EMC 6490 • Decodable Stories and Phonics Activities

Name _____

Word Family
-old

Write **-old** Words

Fill in the circle next to the name of each picture.

1. 
○ sold
○ scold
○ sun

2. 
○ cat
○ hold
○ cold

3. 
○ go
○ gold
○ game

Complete each sentence. Use the words below.

bold   cold   hold   sold   told

1. I will _____ Dad's hand.

2. The teacher _____ me to sit down in my chair.

3. The ice feels _____.

4. Mom _____ our old car.

5. Lee saved a baby. He is _____.

Note: Cut out the slider parts along the dashed lines.
Then slip the word strip through the slider window.

Word Family -old

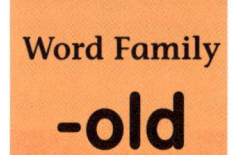

Slide and Read

↑ Pull Up

bold

cold

fold

gold

hold

mold

sold

told

scold

Practice **-old** Words

I know these words!

Hooray!

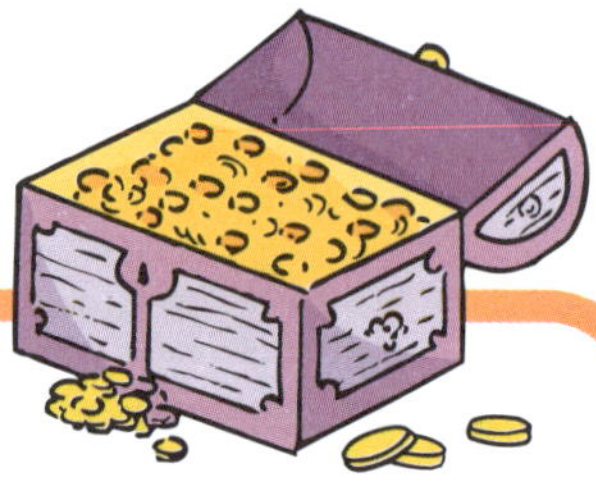

bold
cold
fold
gold
hold
mold
end of -old words
sold
told
scold
fold
cold
bold
hold
gold
mold

Name _____

Word Family
-ow

Learn -ow Words

Words to Know

Write the letters on the lines to make **-ow** words.
Then sound out the words you wrote.

1.  r + ow   ___ ___ ___

2.  t + ow   ___ ___ ___

3.  m + ow   ___ ___ ___

4.  gr + ow   ___ ___ ___ ___

5.  sl + ow   ___ ___ ___ ___

6.  kn + ow   ___ ___ ___ ___

Complete each sentence. Use the words above.

1. Please _____ the grass in the yard.

2. Do you _____ my sister Sally?

3. _____, _____, _____ your boat.

© Evan-Moor Corporation • EMC 6490 • Decodable Stories and Phonics Activities

Story words to know: stuck, boat, pond

Word Family -ow

Name _____

Read -ow Words

Read the story.

I Know

Our car is stuck in the snow.
I know we need a tow.

Our grass will grow and grow.
I know it needs a mow.

Our boat is in the pond.
I know we need to row.

We need a tow,
We need to mow,
We need to row.

I know, I know!

Take the story home. Read it to your family.

Name _____

Word Family
-OW

About "I Know"

Fill in the circle that tells about the story.

1. First?

    ○ car needs a tow
    ○ boat needs a row
    ○ grass needs a mow

2. Next?

    ○ car needs a tow
    ○ boat needs a row
    ○ grass needs a mow

3. Last?

    ○ car needs a tow
    ○ boat needs a row
    ○ grass needs a mow

Draw a line to make a match.

1. car •   • will grow and grow

2. boat •   • stuck in the snow

3. grass •   • in the pond

Name _____

Word Family

-OW

Write **-ow** Words

Fill in the circle next to the name of each picture.

1.
- ○ blow
- ○ black
- ○ bow

2.
- ○ slow
- ○ crow
- ○ glow

3.
- ○ row
- ○ rope
- ○ rose

Complete each sentence. Use the words below.

> blow   grow   know   show   slow

1. Do you _____ how to tell time?

2. The plant will _____ tall if you feed it.

3. Bill likes to _____ bubbles with his gum.

4. Mom can _____ you how to skate.

5. A snail is a _____ animal.

Note: Cut out the slider parts along the dashed lines.
Then slip the word strip through the slider window.

Word Family -ow

Slide and Read

↑ Pull Up

bow

mow

row

tow

blow

crow

glow

grow

know

slow

snow

Practice -ow Words

I know these words!

Hooray!

© Evan-Moor Corporation • EMC 6490 • Decodable Stories and Phonics Activities

77

end of
-ow words

Word Games

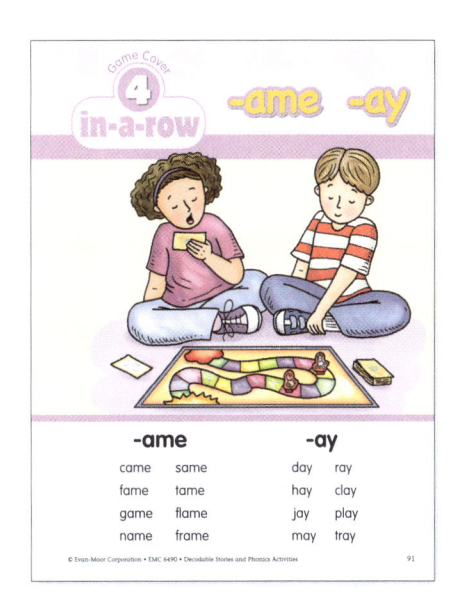

4 in-a-row

-ate -ice

-ate		-ice	
date	crate	dice	rice
gate	plate	lice	price
late	skate	mice	slice
mate	state	nice	twice

-ame -ay

-ame		-ay	
came	same	day	ray
fame	tame	hay	clay
game	flame	jay	play
name	frame	may	tray

-ee -ow

-ee		-ow	
bee	knee	mow	crow
flee	three	row	glow
free	tree	tow	grow
glee	agree	blow	slow

Make It!

Materials Needed for Each Game

- 9" x 12" (23 x 30.5 cm) envelope
- 2 quart-sized, self-locking plastic bags
- scissors
- two-sided tape
- game markers (beans, Quiet Counters, paper squares, etc.)

Steps to Follow

1. Make copies of the picture dictionary for each player. Then make copies of the game boards, one for each player. Laminate all the copies you made.

2. Make one copy of the game cover, caller's cards, and caller's board. Laminate all of them.

3. Tape the laminated cover to the front of the envelope.

4. Cut apart the caller's cards and place them in one of the quart-sized plastic bags.

5. Place counters in the other quart-sized plastic bag.

6. Place all materials inside the 9" x 12" envelope.

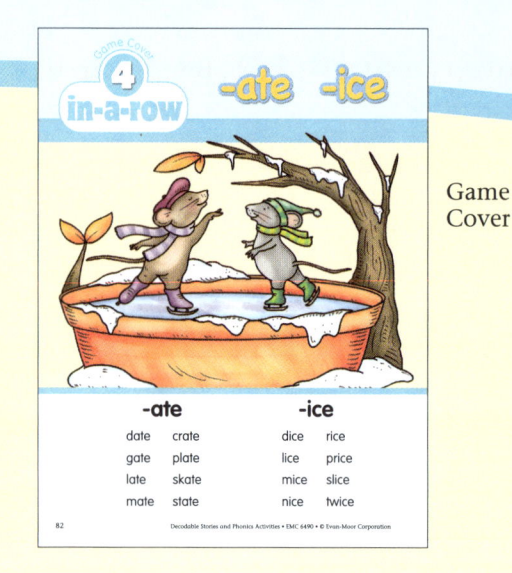

Game Cover

Picture Dictionary

5 Game Boards

Caller's Cards

Caller's Board

Play It!

Object of the game:

Students cover a complete row of words across, down, or diagonally.

1. Select a caller.

2. Distribute a picture dictionary to each player. As a group, have players point to each word and read it aloud. Players may keep the picture dictionary beside them as they play the game.

3. Next, the caller gives each player a game board and some counters.

4. The caller keeps the caller's board and word cards. The caller tells the players that the object of the game is to cover a complete row of words across, down, or diagonally.

5. The caller selects a word card, calls out the word, and places the card on the caller's board.

6. The students find the word on their game boards and cover it with a counter.

7. Play continues until a student covers a complete row of words across, down, or diagonally. The player reads the words aloud as the caller checks the caller's board.

8. Play as many times as time and interest allow. Students may keep the same game board, or the caller may mix up the game boards and redistribute them.

Game Cover 4 in-a-row

-ate   -ice

-ate

date   crate
gate   plate
late   skate
mate   state

-ice

dice   rice
lice   price
mice   slice
nice   twice

Picture Dictionary

-ate

crate

gate

plate

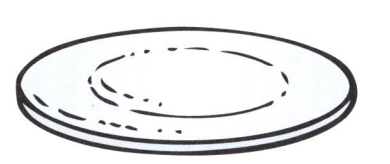

skate

-ice

dice

mice

rice

slice

Game Board 1

-ate

-ice

dice	date	gate	lice
late	mate	mice	nice
twice	crate	plate	rice
state	slice	skate	price

Game Board 2

-ate

-ice

price	rice	mate	dice
date	mice	plate	nice
gate	lice	skate	crate
late	twice	slice	state

Game Board 3

-ate

-ice

skate	slice	twice	late
crate	state	price	rice
mate	dice	date	mice
plate	nice	gate	lice

Game Board 4

-ate

-ice

mate	mice	rice	crate
slice	skate	plate	nice
gate	date	late	twice
state	price	lice	dice

Game Board 5

-ate

-ice

price	rice	nice	gate
lice	mice	plate	skate
state	crate	late	date
dice	mate	twice	slice

Caller's Cards

date	gate	late	mate
crate	plate	skate	state
dice	lice	mice	nice
rice	price	slice	twice

Caller's Board 4 in-a-row

crate	date	gate	late
mate	plate	skate	state
dice	lice	mice	nice
price	rice	slice	twice

Game Cover 4
in-a-row

-ame -ay

-ame

came	same
fame	tame
game	flame
name	frame

-ay

day	ray
hay	clay
jay	play
may	tray

Picture Dictionary

-ame   -ay

flame	clay
frame	hay
game	jay
name	tray

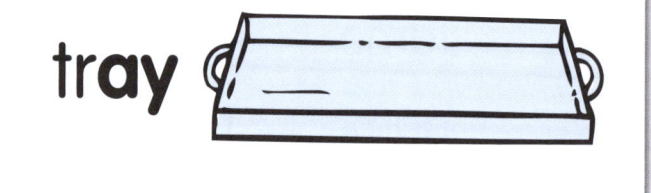

92 Decodable Stories and Phonics Activities • EMC 6490 • © Evan-Moor Corporation

Game Board 1

-ame   -ay

came	day	hay	tame
tray	play	flame	game
jay	fame	may	clay
same	ray	frame	name

Game Board 2

-ame

-ay

name	flame	play	came
day	may	clay	game
hay	tame	frame	fame
tray	jay	ray	same

94 Decodable Stories and Phonics Activities • EMC 6490 • © Evan-Moor Corporation

Game Board 3

-ame

-ay

same	fame	flame	tame
hay	play	jay	frame
day	came	ray	may
game	name	clay	tray

© Evan-Moor Corporation • EMC 6490 • Decodable Stories and Phonics Activities

Game Board 4

-ame

-ay

play	flame	may	fame
ray	day	clay	game
hay	frame	tray	jay
same	name	tame	came

Game Board 5

-ame

-ay

same	jay	tray	came
ray	fame	play	day
frame	may	flame	hay
name	clay	game	tame

Caller's Cards

came	fame	game	name
same	tame	flame	frame
day	hay	jay	may
ray	clay	play	tray

Caller's Board 4 in-a-row

came	fame	flame	frame
game	name	same	tame
clay	day	hay	jay
may	play	ray	tray

Game Cover 4 in-a-row

-ee -ow

-ee

bee	knee
flee	three
free	tree
glee	agree

-ow

mow	crow
row	glow
tow	grow
blow	slow

100 Decodable Stories and Phonics Activities • EMC 6490 • © Evan-Moor Corporation

Picture Dictionary

-ee

b**ee**

kn**ee**

thr**ee**

tr**ee**

-ow

bl**ow**

cr**ow**

m**ow**

t**ow**

Game Board 1

-ee   -ow

bee	row	slow	free
tow	crow	mow	glee
blow	grow	three	flee
agree	knee	glow	tree

Game Board 2

-ee

-ow

crow	agree	bee	mow
tree	tow	glee	grow
three	knee	slow	blow
glow	free	flee	row

Game Board 3

-ee   -ow

free	blow	three	tow
row	bee	crow	tree
knee	mow	glee	slow
glow	agree	grow	flee

Game Board 4

-ee   -ow

mow	flee	grow	tree
agree	row	three	tow
glow	glee	blow	knee
bee	crow	free	slow

Game Board 5

-ee   -ow

three	slow	bee	blow
glee	crow	flee	row
knee	tow	tree	grow
agree	glow	free	mow

Caller's Cards

bee	knee	three	tree
free	glee	flee	agree
crow	mow	row	blow
grow	slow	tow	glow

Caller's Board 4 in-a-row

agree	bee	flee	free
glee	knee	three	tree
blow	crow	glow	grow
mow	row	slow	tow

Answer Key

Page 9

About "A Day of Fun"

Circle the word that tells about the story. Then write the word on the line.

1. Form a blue jay with **clay** — (clay)
2. Jump in the **hay** — (hay)
3. Use a hose to **spray** — (spray)
4. **Play** some music. — (Play)
5. Dance and **sway** to the music. — (sway)

Fill in the circle next to the correct answer.

1. What is a good name for the story?
   - ● A Day to Play
2. Where is the hay?
   - ● in the barn
3. What is a word that means you are happy?
   - ● hooray

Page 10

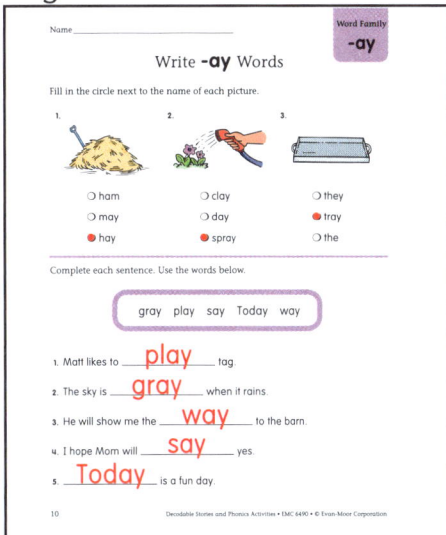

Write -ay Words

Fill in the circle next to the name of each picture.

1. ● hay
2. ● spray
3. ● tray

Complete each sentence. Use the words below.

gray play say Today way

1. Matt likes to **play** tag.
2. The sky is **gray** when it rains.
3. He will show me the **way** to the barn.
4. I hope Mom will **say** yes.
5. **Today** is a fun day.

Page 15

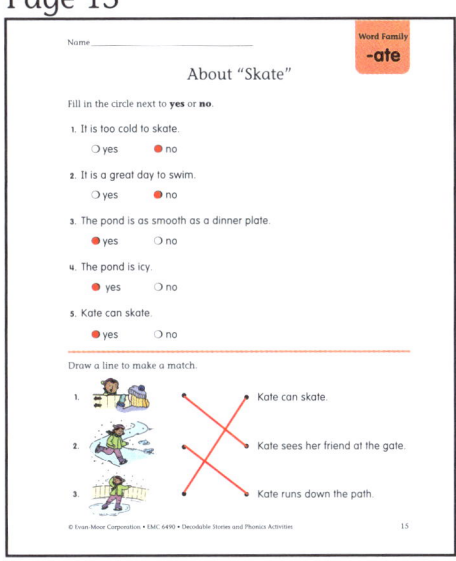

About "Skate"

Fill in the circle next to yes or no.

1. It is too cold to skate. — ● no
2. It is a great day to swim. — ● no
3. The pond is as smooth as a dinner plate. — ● yes
4. The pond is icy. — ● yes
5. Kate can skate. — ● yes

Draw a line to make a match.

1. — Kate can skate.
2. — Kate sees her friend at the gate.
3. — Kate runs down the path.

Page 16

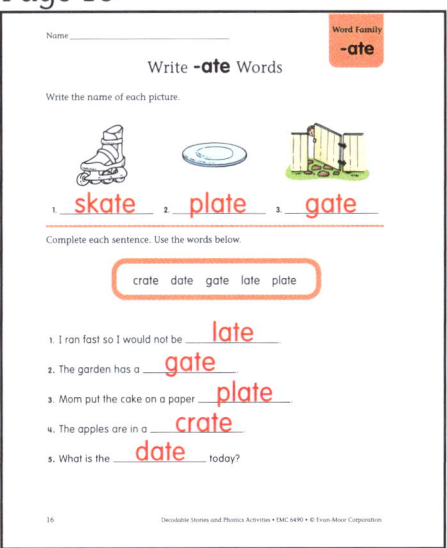

Write -ate Words

Write the name of each picture.

1. skate
2. plate
3. gate

Complete each sentence. Use the words below.

crate date gate late plate

1. I ran fast so I would not be **late**.
2. The garden has a **gate**.
3. Mom put the cake on a paper **plate**.
4. The apples are in a **crate**.
5. What is the **date** today?

Page 21

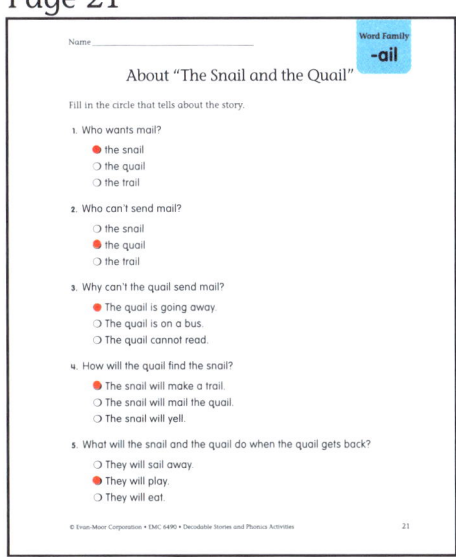

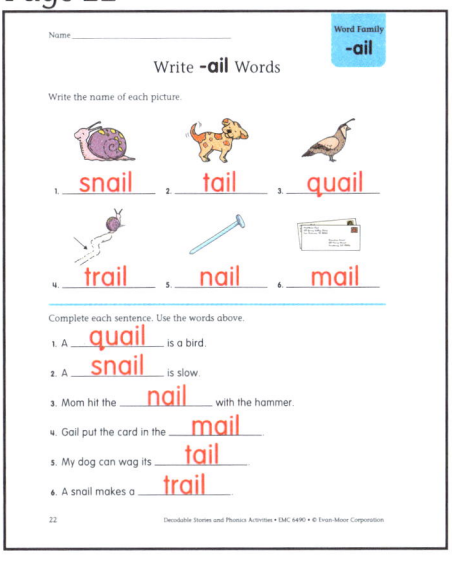

About "The Snail and the Quail"

Fill in the circle that tells about the story.

1. Who wants mail?
   - ● the snail
2. Who can't send mail?
   - ● the quail
3. Why can't the quail send mail?
   - ● The quail is going away.
4. How will the quail find the snail?
   - ● The snail will make a trail.
5. What will the snail and the quail do when the quail gets back?
   - ● They will play.

Page 22

Write -ail Words

Write the name of each picture.

1. snail
2. tail
3. quail
4. trail
5. nail
6. mail

Complete each sentence. Use the words above.

1. A **quail** is a bird.
2. A **snail** is slow.
3. Mom hit the **nail** with the hammer.
4. Gail put the card in the **mail**.
5. My dog can wag its **tail**.
6. A snail makes a **trail**.

© Evan-Moor Corporation • EMC 6490 • Decodable Stories and Phonics Activities

109

Page 27

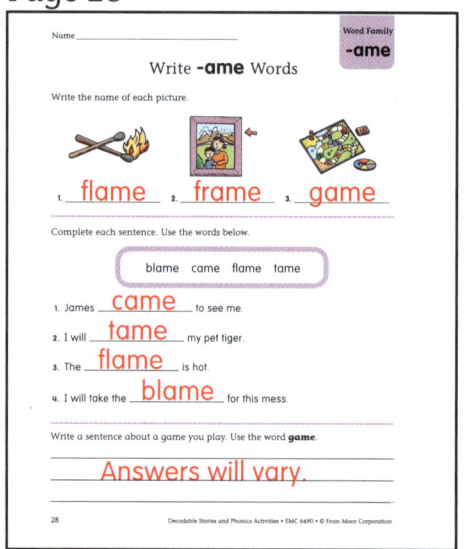

About "The Game"

Fill in the circle that tells about the story.

1. What is the story about?
   - ○ James sings.
   - ● James makes up games.
   - ○ James does not like to play games.

2. What does James do to the bears?
   - ○ James names the bears.
   - ○ James feeds the bears.
   - ● James tames the bears.

3. James sees a flame. He _____
   - ○ watches the fire
   - ● puts out the fire
   - ○ puts a log on the fire

4. Where does James put his art?
   - ○ in a box
   - ● in a frame
   - ○ on the wall

5. Which one tells about James?
   - ○ James is old.
   - ○ James is sad.
   - ● James is fun.

Word Family: -ame

Page 28

Write -ame Words

Write the name of each picture.

1. flame
2. frame
3. game

Complete each sentence. Use the words below.

blame   came   flame   tame

1. James **came** to see me.
2. I will **tame** my pet tiger.
3. The **flame** is hot.
4. I will take the **blame** for this mess.

Write a sentence about a game you play. Use the word **game**.

Answers will vary.

Word Family: -ame

Page 33

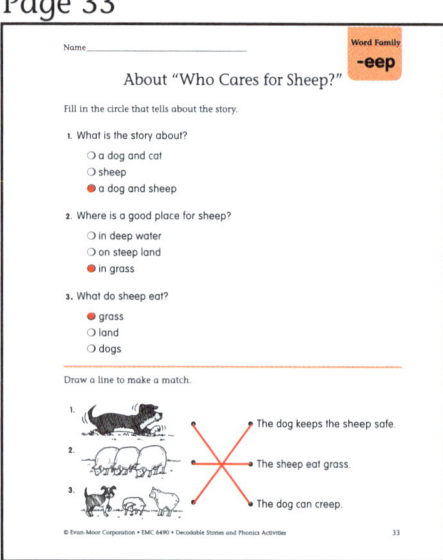

About "Who Cares for Sheep?"

Fill in the circle that tells about the story.

1. What is the story about?
   - ○ a dog and cat
   - ○ sheep
   - ● a dog and sheep

2. Where is a good place for sheep?
   - ○ in deep water
   - ○ on steep land
   - ● in grass

3. What do sheep eat?
   - ● grass
   - ○ land
   - ○ dogs

Draw a line to make a match.

1. — The dog keeps the sheep safe.
2. — The sheep eat grass.
3. — The dog can creep.

Word Family: -eep

Page 34

Write -eep Words

Write the name of each picture.

1. sleep
2. creep
3. jeep
4. sweep
5. sheep
6. steep

Complete each sentence. Use the words below.

deep   keep   sheep   sweep

1. The dog cares for the **sheep**.
2. Mom and Dad **keep** me safe.
3. Jen will **sweep** away the dirt.
4. Jon does not swim in **deep** water.

Word Family: -eep

Page 39

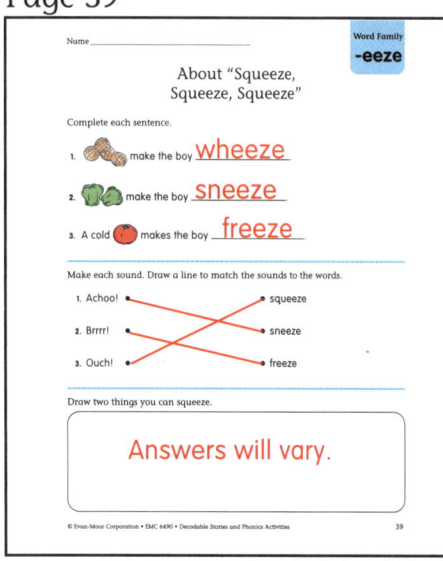

About "Squeeze, Squeeze, Squeeze"

Complete each sentence.

1. 🥜 make the boy **wheeze**
2. 🥦 make the boy **sneeze**
3. A cold 🔴 makes the boy **freeze**

Make each sound. Draw a line to match the sounds to the words.

1. Achoo! — sneeze
2. Brrrr! — freeze
3. Ouch! — squeeze

Draw two things you can squeeze.

Answers will vary.

Word Family: -eeze

Page 40

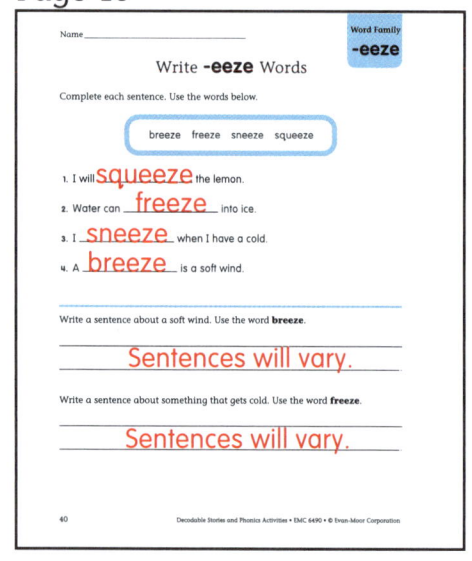

Write -eeze Words

Complete each sentence. Use the words below.

breeze   freeze   sneeze   squeeze

1. I will **squeeze** the lemon.
2. Water can **freeze** into ice.
3. I **sneeze** when I have a cold.
4. A **breeze** is a soft wind.

Write a sentence about a soft wind. Use the word **breeze**.

Sentences will vary.

Write a sentence about something that gets cold. Use the word **freeze**.

Sentences will vary.

Word Family: -eeze

110 Decodable Stories and Phonics Activities • EMC 6490 • © Evan-Moor Corporation

Page 45

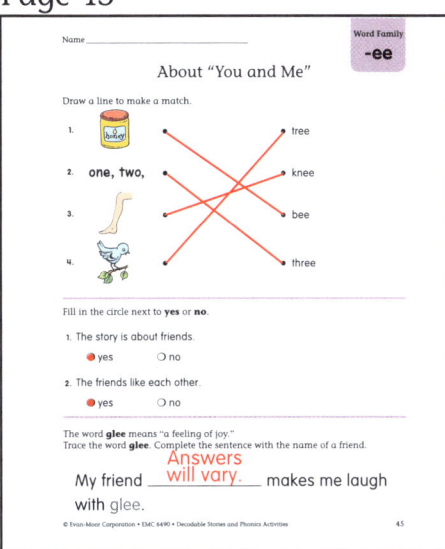

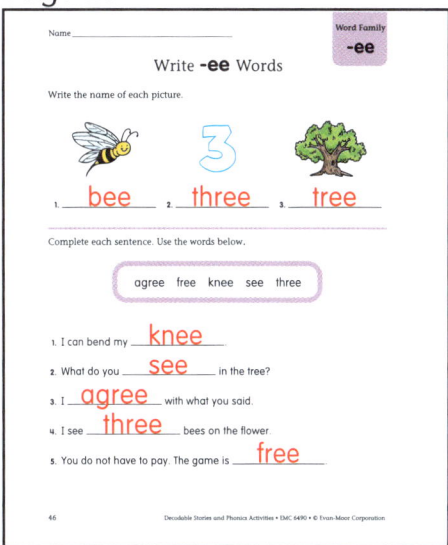

About "You and Me"
Word Family: -ee

Draw a line to make a match.
1. honey → bee
2. one, two, → three
3. knee (leg) → knee
4. bird → tree

Fill in the circle next to **yes** or **no**.
1. The story is about friends. ● yes ○ no
2. The friends like each other. ● yes ○ no

The word **glee** means "a feeling of joy."
Trace the word **glee**. Complete the sentence with the name of a friend.

My friend _Answers will vary._ makes me laugh with glee.

Page 46

Write -ee Words
Word Family: -ee

Write the name of each picture.
1. bee
2. three
3. tree

Complete each sentence. Use the words below.
[agree free knee see three]

1. I can bend my __knee__.
2. What do you __see__ in the tree?
3. I __agree__ with what you said.
4. I see __three__ bees on the flower.
5. You do not have to pay. The game is __free__.

Page 51

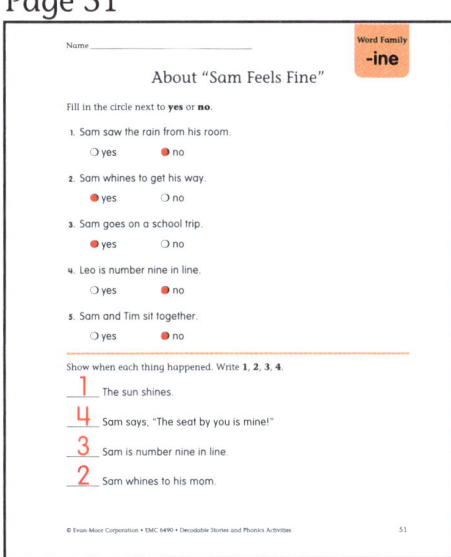

About "Sam Feels Fine"
Word Family: -ine

Fill in the circle next to **yes** or **no**.
1. Sam saw the rain from his room. ○ yes ● no
2. Sam whines to get his way. ● yes ○ no
3. Sam goes on a school trip. ● yes ○ no
4. Leo is number nine in line. ○ yes ● no
5. Sam and Tim sit together. ● yes ○ no

Show when each thing happened. Write **1**, **2**, **3**, **4**.
_1_ The sun shines.
_4_ Sam says, "The seat by you is mine!"
_3_ Sam is number nine in line.
_2_ Sam whines to his mom.

Page 52

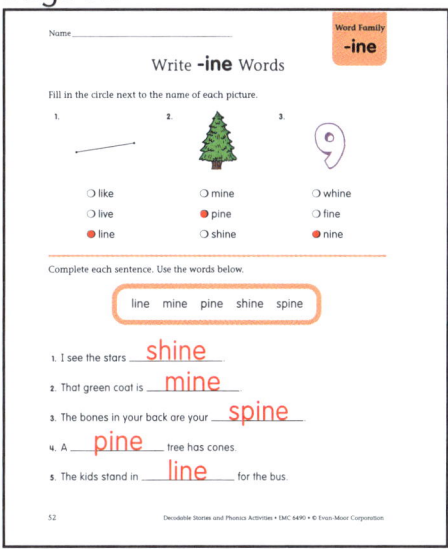

Write -ine Words
Word Family: -ine

Fill in the circle next to the name of each picture.
1. ○ like ○ live ● line
2. ○ mine ● pine ○ shine
3. ○ whine ○ fine ● nine

Complete each sentence. Use the words below.
[line mine pine shine spine]

1. I see the stars __shine__.
2. That green coat is __mine__.
3. The bones in your back are your __spine__.
4. A __pine__ tree has cones.
5. The kids stand in __line__ for the bus.

Page 57

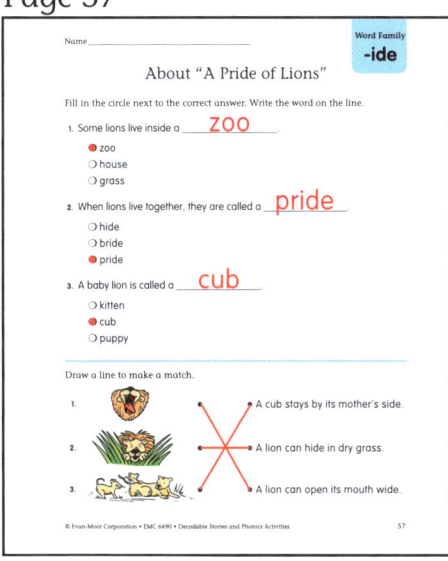

About "A Pride of Lions"
Word Family: -ide

Fill in the circle next to the correct answer. Write the word on the line.
1. Some lions live inside a __zoo__.
   ● zoo ○ house ○ grass
2. When lions live together, they are called a __pride__.
   ○ hide ○ bride ● pride
3. A baby lion is called a __cub__.
   ○ kitten ● cub ○ puppy

Draw a line to make a match.
1. lion face → A lion can open its mouth wide.
2. lion in grass → A lion can hide in dry grass.
3. cubs → A cub stays by its mother's side.

Page 58

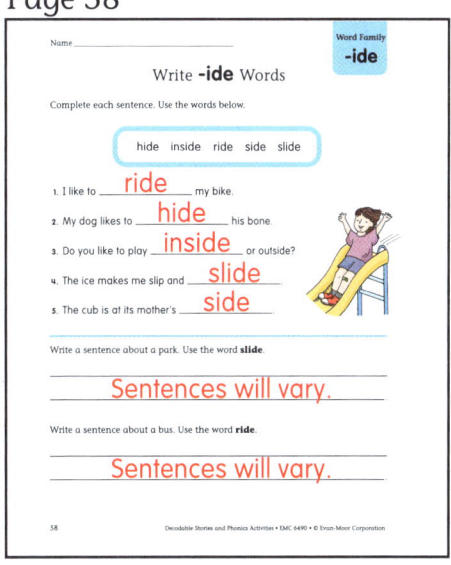

Write -ide Words
Word Family: -ide

Complete each sentence. Use the words below.
[hide inside ride side slide]

1. I like to __ride__ my bike.
2. My dog likes to __hide__ his bone.
3. Do you like to play __inside__ or outside?
4. The ice makes me slip and __slide__.
5. The cub is at its mother's __side__.

Write a sentence about a park. Use the word **slide**.
Sentences will vary.

Write a sentence about a bus. Use the word **ride**.
Sentences will vary.

Page 63

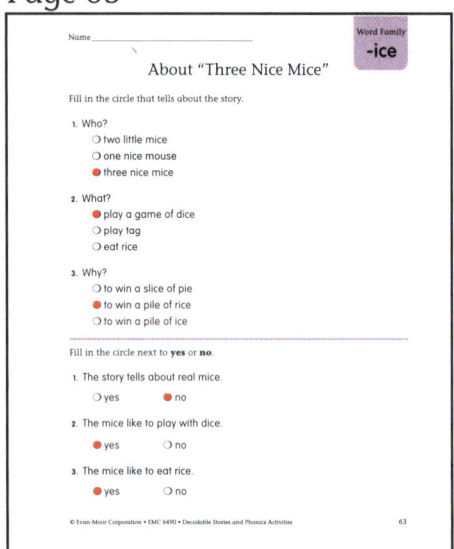

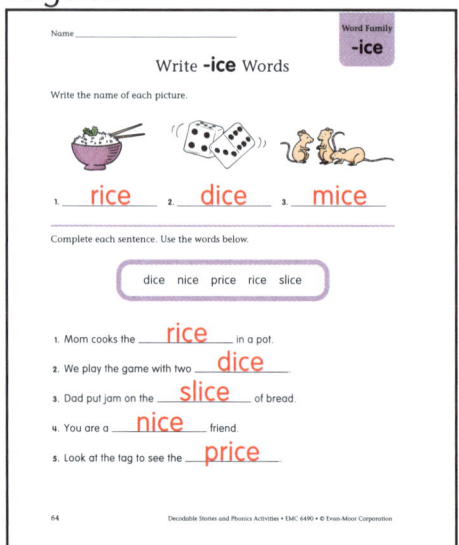

About "Three Nice Mice"

Fill in the circle that tells about the story.

1. Who?
   - ○ two little mice
   - ○ one nice mouse
   - ● three nice mice

2. What?
   - ● play a game of dice
   - ○ play tag
   - ○ eat rice

3. Why?
   - ○ to win a slice of pie
   - ● to win a pile of rice
   - ○ to win a pile of ice

Fill in the circle next to **yes** or **no**.

1. The story tells about real mice.
   - ○ yes   ● no
2. The mice like to play with dice.
   - ● yes   ○ no
3. The mice like to eat rice.
   - ● yes   ○ no

Page 64

Write -ice Words

Write the name of each picture.

1. rice   2. dice   3. mice

Complete each sentence. Use the words below.

> dice nice price rice slice

1. Mom cooks the **rice** in a pot.
2. We play the game with two **dice**.
3. Dad put jam on the **slice** of bread.
4. You are a **nice** friend.
5. Look at the tag to see the **price**.

Page 69

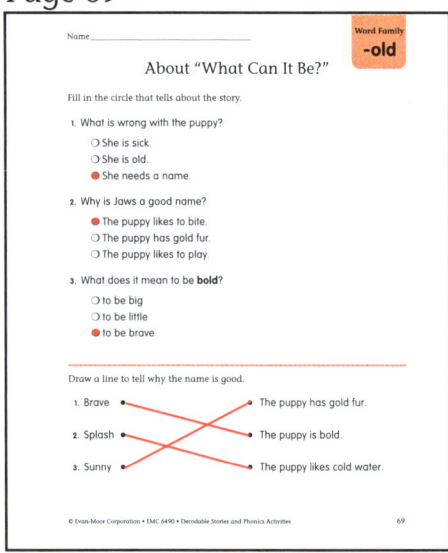

About "What Can It Be?"

Fill in the circle that tells about the story.

1. What is wrong with the puppy?
   - ○ She is sick.
   - ○ She is old.
   - ● She needs a name.

2. Why is Jaws a good name?
   - ● The puppy likes to bite.
   - ○ The puppy has gold fur.
   - ○ The puppy likes to play.

3. What does it mean to be **bold**?
   - ○ to be big
   - ○ to be little
   - ● to be brave

Draw a line to tell why the name is good.

1. Brave — The puppy is bold.
2. Splash — The puppy likes cold water.
3. Sunny — The puppy has gold fur.

Page 70

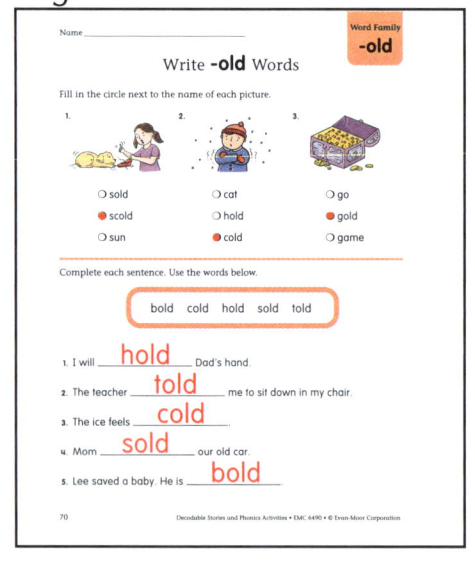

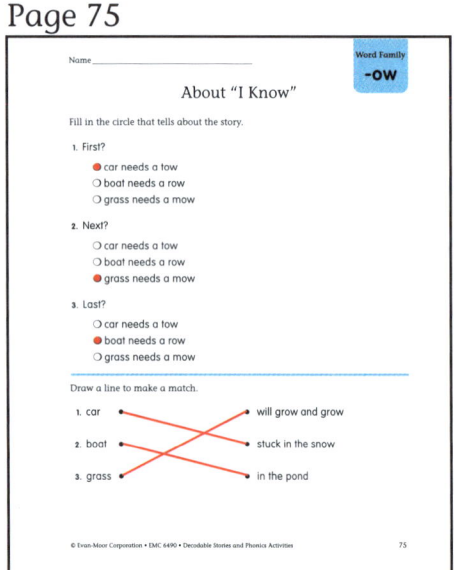

Write -old Words

Fill in the circle next to the name of each picture.

1. ○ sold ● scold ○ sun
2. ○ cat ○ hold ● cold
3. ○ go ● gold ○ game

Complete each sentence. Use the words below.

> bold cold hold sold told

1. I will **hold** Dad's hand.
2. The teacher **told** me to sit down in my chair.
3. The ice feels **cold**.
4. Mom **sold** our old car.
5. Lee saved a baby. He is **bold**.

Page 75

About "I Know"

Fill in the circle that tells about the story.

1. First?
   - ● car needs a tow
   - ○ boat needs a row
   - ○ grass needs a mow

2. Next?
   - ○ car needs a tow
   - ○ boat needs a row
   - ● grass needs a mow

3. Last?
   - ○ car needs a tow
   - ● boat needs a row
   - ○ grass needs a mow

Draw a line to make a match.

1. car — stuck in the snow
2. boat — in the pond
3. grass — will grow and grow

Page 76

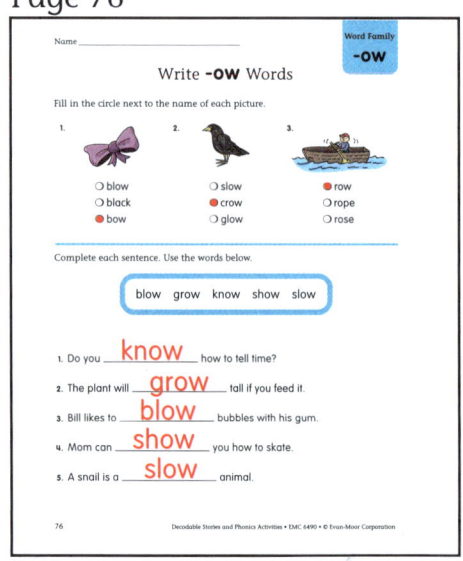

Write -ow Words

Fill in the circle next to the name of each picture.

1. ○ blow ○ black ● bow
2. ○ slow ● crow ○ glow
3. ● row ○ rope ○ rose

Complete each sentence. Use the words below.

> blow grow know show slow

1. Do you **know** how to tell time?
2. The plant will **grow** tall if you feed it.
3. Bill likes to **blow** bubbles with his gum.
4. Mom can **show** you how to skate.
5. A snail is a **slow** animal.